When My Soul Bleeds Words

a poetry collection by

LEAH K OXENDINE

WHEN MY SOUL BLEEDS WORDS
By Leah K. Oxendine

Photography by Mikalia Flood
Cover design by Brian McBride
Cover photo by Mikalia Flood
All illustrations by Leah K. Oxendine

ISBN: 978-0-578-40232-1

praise

"Sometimes traditional and sometimes freestyle, Ms. Miller's poetry has something for everyone. Her italicized wisdom-thoughts are sparkling, and her own illustrations are spot-on visuals of her poems. The book begins in pits of darkness, but ends in rays of God's glorious light. I recommend ***When My Soul Bleeds Words*** for anyone struggling with themselves and life; you aren't alone." - *Sheridan E. Claude, author and screenwriter*

"***When My Soul Bleeds Words*** is a beautiful collection of poetry and prose depicting the thought-life of a young girl learning to understand and discover purpose. Full of pithy gems, moving expressions and beautiful artwork it's easy to feel and connect with the author. If you enjoy deep poetry that expresses real emotions, you'll love this." - *Keturah Lamb, author and blogger*

"A vulnerable, raw, yet hopeful look into the heart of the author as she pens many of the hurts we all push down yet crave for others to understand." - *Doctor Raymond Force*

"***When My Soul Bleeds Words*** is an honest look at what it means to be human. Even more, what it means to have faith in the midst of raw, broken humanity. This collection is raw and real. It doesn't shy away from hard truths and, in the end, it fills you with the hope that though we may be broken, healing is on its way." - *Brian McBride, author of* Love and the Sea and Everything in Between

index

To the only One who has truly ever understood the vivid chaos of my inner self.

To the only Being that I knew would never abandon me, even in my times of mental and emotional desolation.

To the One that saved my life, the One that saved me from myself.

To Jesus Christ, my Lord, Savior, Creator and friend.

Also, in memory of my unborn daughter, Hope, miscarried on 9/28/18.
See you in Heaven, my little one.

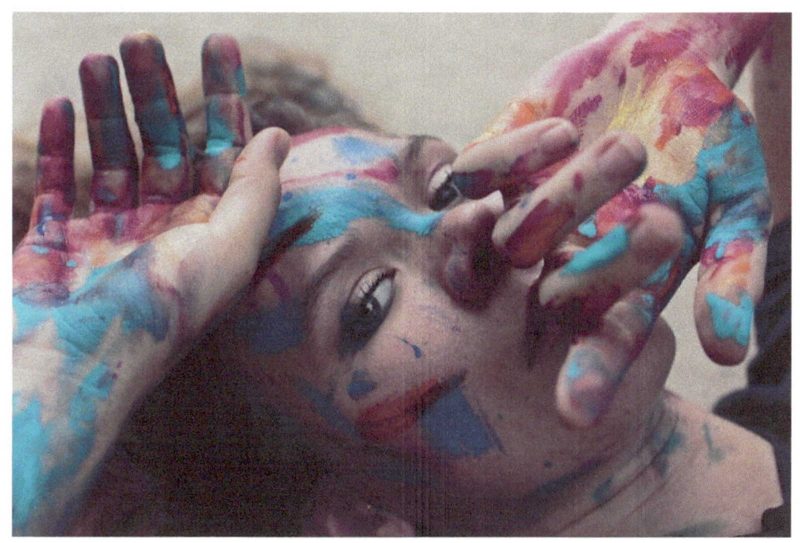

prologue

What does it truly mean to be human? When we peel back this outer shell of flesh and blood, what do we find, other than organs and tissue? Humanity's essence is trapped in the soul, which is a thing none of us can scientifically label. The human soul is a mystery beyond the comprehension of labs and test tubes. It simply exists as it is.

They tell us to not judge a book by its cover, nor a person by his or her outer appearance. In 1 Samuel 16:7 it says "…For man looks at the outward appearance, but God looks at the heart." Our bodies are only vehicles—mere tools for us to portray what goes on in the soul. The soul is what gives us our individualism, our need to be loved, and our need to understand why everything happens as it does.

Yet the human soul is a thing of calamity. It is sometimes the worst foe you will ever meet. It will cause you the deepest pain, and betray you the quickest. It is not to be trusted. At the same time, it is full of potential beauty and immense depth. It can be the spring from whence flows visions and dreams, or the pit that ensnares many a lost and confused mind. The human soul was designed for fellowship and communion, first with God, and then with mankind.

This book exists for several reasons, but the main one is because I wanted to tell the world a different story about the struggle of being human. A different perspective on the soul and its many vibrant colors of emotion and feeling. What it is like to battle your own mind, day to day, and still try to appear sane to the outside world. But most importantly, what it's like to fall down time and time again, and still find redemption and reconciliation in the end.

This book is my own story. My journey. My battle with mental illness, depression and even suicidal tendencies. It is told through artwork, as well as words. The poetry spans several years of my recent life, starting at about age eighteen. You see, my way of coping with hardships or pain was to write about it. I found a sense of limited release in being able to jot down what I was experiencing. At the time, I didn't think I would ever show anyone. But as I've gotten older, and have recovered from my past, I know that I am supposed to share these pieces of my heart with you.

As a child of the King of Kings, I am washed in Jesus' blood and made new in Him. But part of why I decided to compile this book was because I wanted to remind the world of something that many people tend to forget. As a Christian, I am far from perfect. I have struggled through temptations and hardships, like anyone else. I've stumbled and backslid. I've hated myself. I've wanted to die. I have longed to put an end to it all. I have cried out to God, begging Him to save me from the chaos and the voices in my head. And I have sobbed myself to sleep, wondering why He did not take the unexplained heartache away.

In essence, I have experienced both the darkness and light of being human, in my own little limited perspective. Being a Christian is not the world's definition of easy. Sometimes trusting God and obeying Him is the hardest thing you can do. And sometimes He lets us suffer through things we don't understand.

So basically, I wrote this book to remind the world that Christians are still human, and we still bleed. We still experience pain. The only difference is we serve the Creator of the Universe and He is our Rock and Salvation. Because of that, we are not alone.

He heard my prayers, by the way. Even though I didn't see it at the time.

And He did save me from myself.

It has been almost two years since I've had a panic attack or severe bipolar mood swing. I used to think that I was a monster, an alien and not worthy to breathe. I heard sounds and voices in my head that weren't really there. It was terrifying. But you know what? God is more powerful than my mind or the chemical imbalances in my brain. And I am stronger now for experiencing everything that I have.

the secret realm of reality

PART I

bullet holes

My heart's riddled with bullet holes;
Shots I fired myself, my own fault.

With my own knife I cut in deep;
I take pleasure in the pain as I slowly bleed.

The choices I make haunt my soul;
But I decide to not care, to freeze my conscience cold.

Self-inflicted fractures, punctures, wounds;
Everything that's bad for me I want to do.

Yes, I realize I caused my own pain;
And for these scars I'm the one to blame.

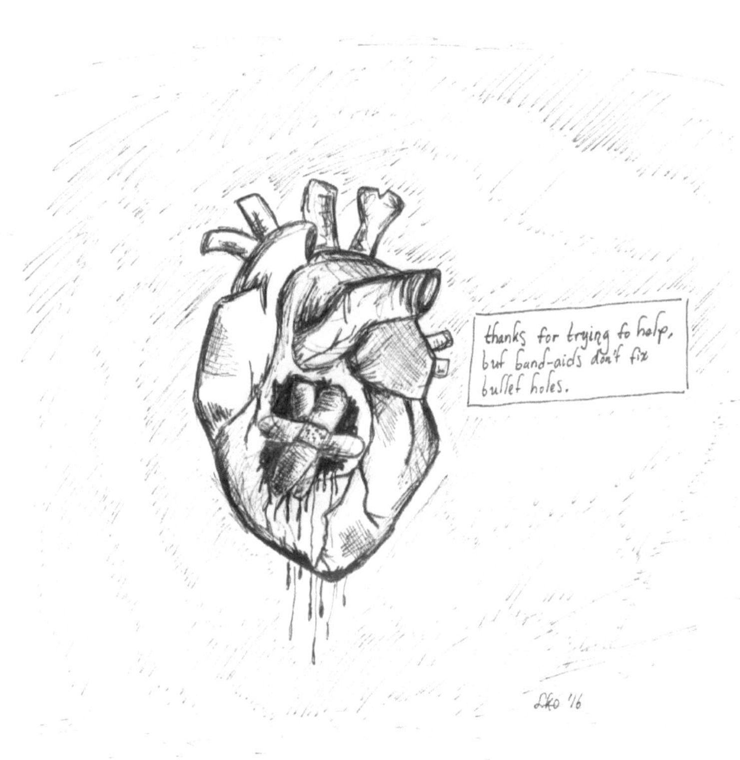
thanks for trying to help,
but band-aids don't fix
bullet holes.

static

The darkness speaks my name,
Showing up like the foe I never asked for.
The chaos drives me insane,
Defiling me with murky water and war.

Voices,
echoes,
shouts,
a din,
Rip me to shreds down deep within.
Give me rest from this burden of calamity,
Father,
break the static,
give me clarity.

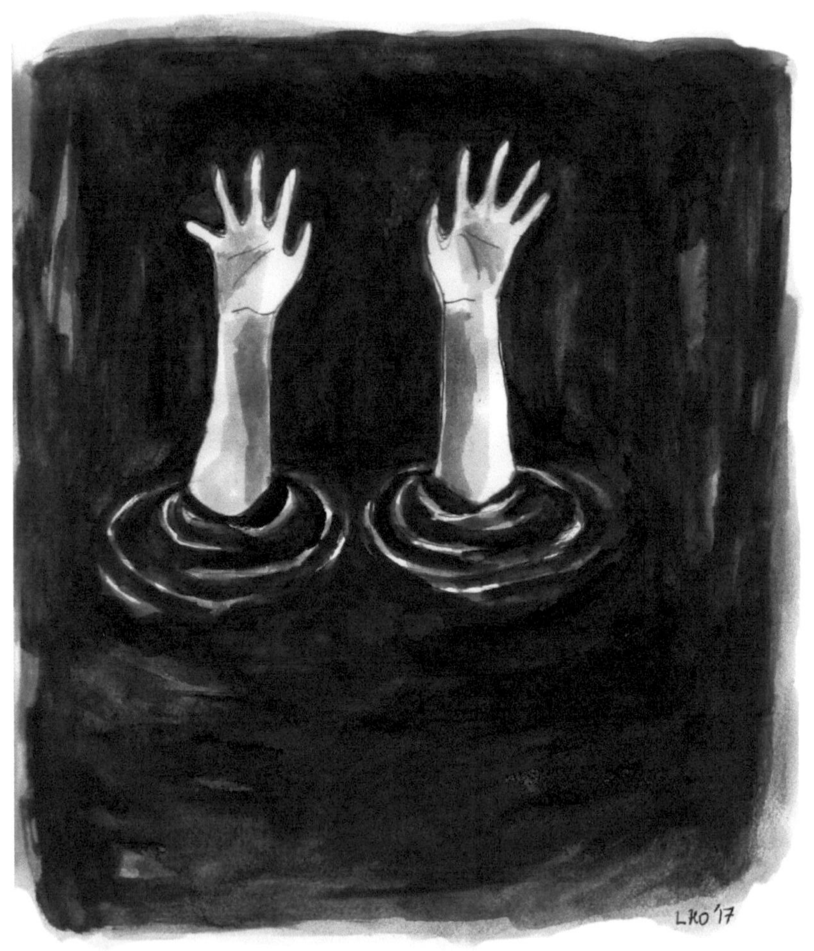
LKO '17

muddy water

Sometimes, you feel dead,
But you don’t know why.

You feel numb,
but it still hurts to cry.

Sometimes, your heart keeps beating,
And your lungs keep breathing,

But you don’t truly feel alive.

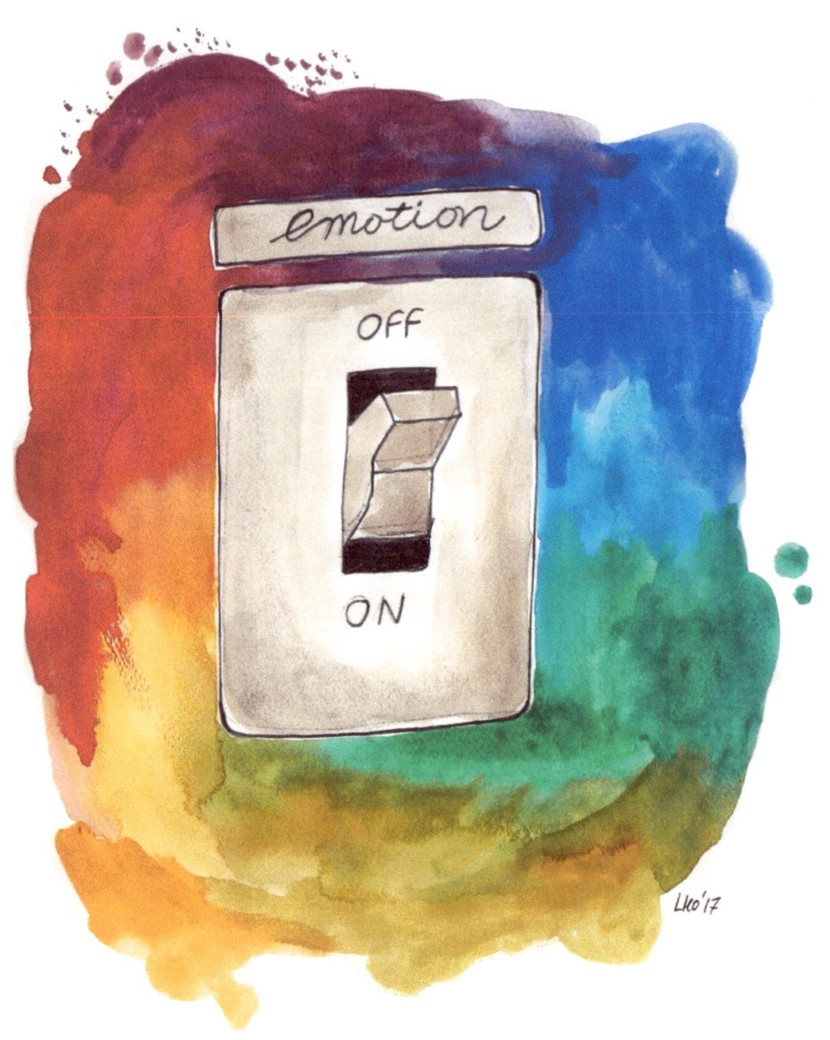
emotion
OFF
ON
LKO'17

drama

The tears roll down her face;
She hates the drama she creates.

Her heart burns with pain she can't understand;
All she wants is just to get with the plan.

But that's the problem – she doesn't know;
What the plan is, which way to go.

It's painful to hold it in, to not let it out;
But it's painful to vent it, to flaunt it about.

Worst of all is never quite knowing
If it's another's fault, or just her doing;

If it's an illness that can be fixed or cured,
With this internal war she can never be sure.

wretched without you

Oh Lord, I am sick,
My mind is confused.
My outlook is tainted,
By things which aren't true.

My head is spinning in a million directions;
I'm lost in the mess of my own imaginations.
And tears are rolling down my face.
Guess I've said enough to rest my case.

I'm lost…
please find me.
I'm falling…
please catch me.
I'm blind…
please enlighten me.
I'm drifting…
please rescue me.

I'm a soldier in retreat,
A warrior in defeat.
I'm broken, I'm fallen,
I've forsaken your calling.

Lord, you know I'm such a mess,
Lost in a swath of filthiness.
Disaster is my name,
And every day it is the same.

It’s all gone so wrong;
The pain never seems to move on.
Lord, I’m begging for an answer,
A rescue, a deliverer.

forbidden feast

Longing for something I can't have,
Unquenchable desires driving me mad.
Lust for physical satisfaction,
And all the wrong kinds of attraction.

Torture to my body and my brain,
A powerful hunger driving me insane.
An incurable affliction, infectious disease,
The demands of my desire are impossible to appease

I feel like an animal starving for meat,
Wanting a fruit I'm forbidden to eat.
Fighting a relentless craving for what's taboo,
The more I fight, the more it rises anew.

Oh God, this need, it never goes away,
And this is how you made me, so what do I say?
Either take from me this desire, make me numb and at peace,
Or provide me satisfaction, let me dine at the forbidden feast.

sometimes i wonder

Sometimes I wonder what would happen
If I ran out into the street,
If I ran out in front of a passing car.

Sometimes I wonder what would happen
If I held my head underwater too long,
If I allowed the water into my lungs.

Sometimes I wonder what would happen
If I took that pair of scissors,
If I plunged the blades into my flesh.

Sometimes I wonder what would happen
If I simply got tired of fighting,
If I simply decided to end.

a dragon locked in a birdcage

Can you hear the throb of her aching heart?
Can you see the hunger in her burning eyes?
I doubt any soul would dare to understand
The desires of a dragon locked in a birdcage.

She fights to not be controlled by her lust,
She longs to be caressed, she aches to be filled.
Yet those things she can tell no one;
Her mind is locked up, how she seeks to be released.

quench the fire

My stomach is lurching, my heart pounds,
Apparently I thought I was strong.
Guess what? I let my guard down.

I'm playing the drama queen,
It hurts to admit the truth.
But just look me in the eyes, you'll see.

I can't believe I opened the door,
I'm not as invincible as I thought.
Like waves on a mighty ocean, the emotions inside me roar.

Abba Father, guide my soul,
Let your will alone be done.
I'm being melodramatic; this is just how life rolls.

I refuse to give into my desire,
To let my heart rage and surge.
Emotion is my greatest enemy, and I will quench this fire.

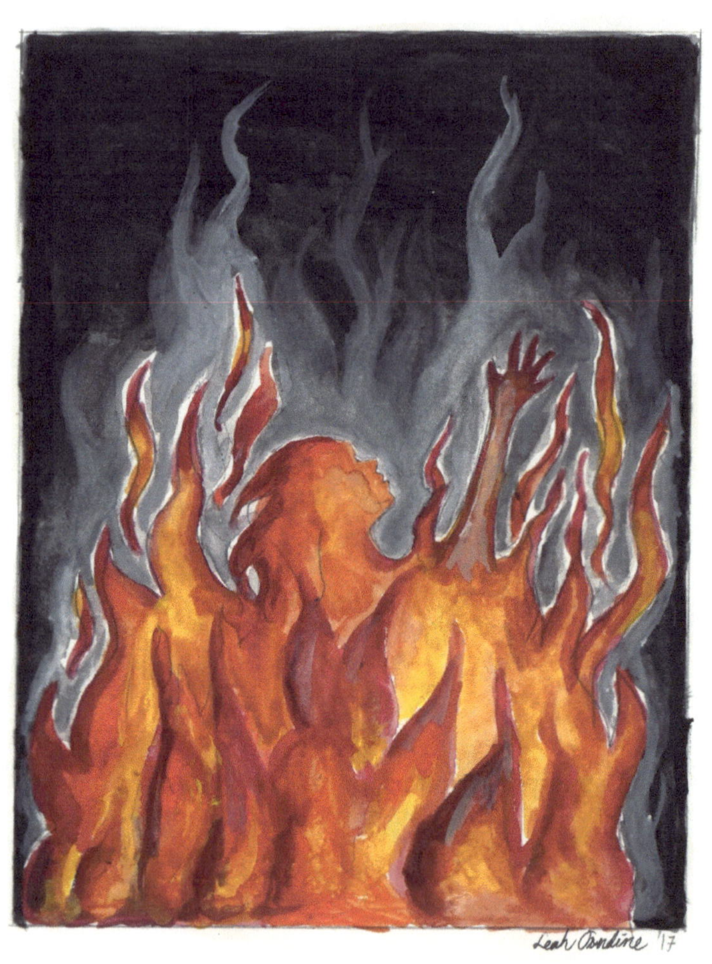

what is love

Dive in headfirst, or lightly tread?
Can only see one step ahead.
I'm disoriented and confused,
How can one know when love is true?

what depression feels like

Inside me is a darkened hole,
In which used to be my soul.
I'm not so sure what's in there now,
Other than the hollowness and doubt.

Some days I am only numb,
I feel devoid of all hope and love.
I've turned into an endless black hole,
My thoughts have become blacker than coal.

A swath of gray swirls around my head,
A permanent cloud of emptiness.
A weight tied to my feet, pulling me down,
Deeper into the slough, soon I will drown.

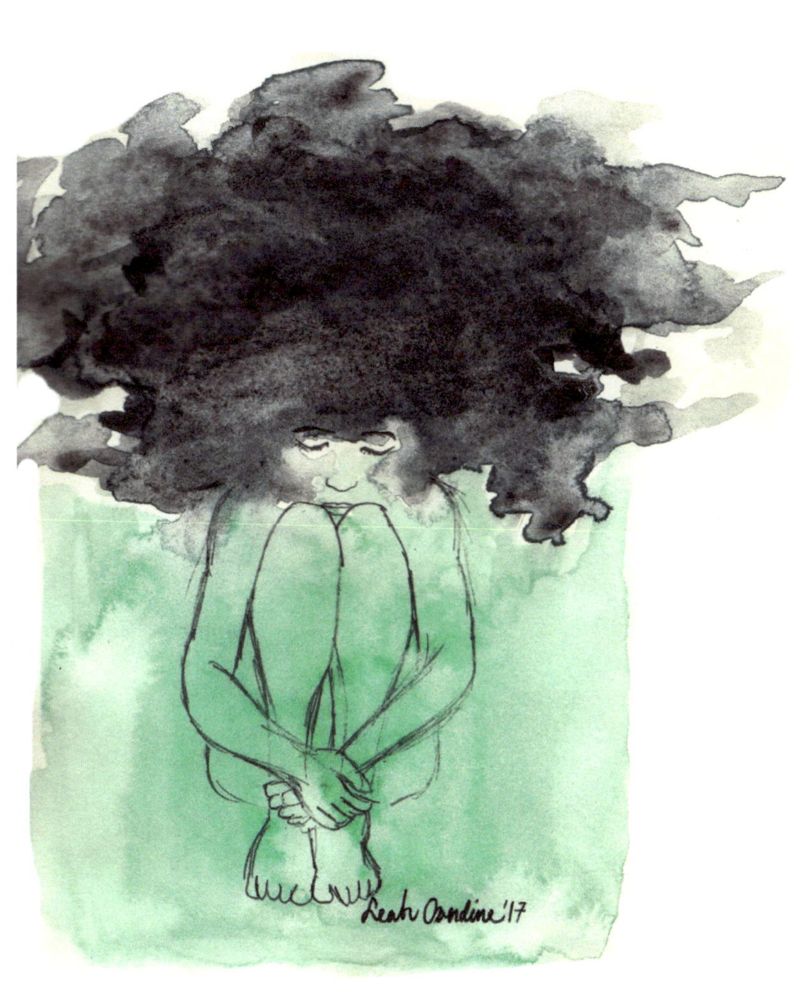
Leah Ondine '17

a fruitless escape

Aching for hands to caress my skin,
My soul cries out for affection and warmth.
Burning with the need to be touched,
I find my mind wandering to things it shouldn't.

I touch myself when no one's looking,
Pretending that my hands are not my own.
For a moment, I do not feel quite so lonely,
But it is only for a moment.

I try to escape to another place,
Using my imagination as a means of transportation.
But like a vapor, the pleasure fades,
And then only the emptiness remains.

therapy

Her silhouette falls across the concrete floor;
She looks out at the ocean and her heart sighs ever more.

She runs out of that motel room away from her family;
Trying to escape, she longs for aloneness, for serenity.

She can't let them see her for what she is, a freak;
According to the voices inside, it's better for her to leave.

The waves knock at her mind, trying to open her heart;
The ocean provides therapy, but it can only do so much.

a prayer

Lord, you are my command;
Please show me your plan.

How will you reveal to me
Your will and mystery?

The mystery of what's in store,
And what leads beyond this door?

How will you show me what's ahead?
Or will you keep it from me instead?

the restoration & refining

PART II

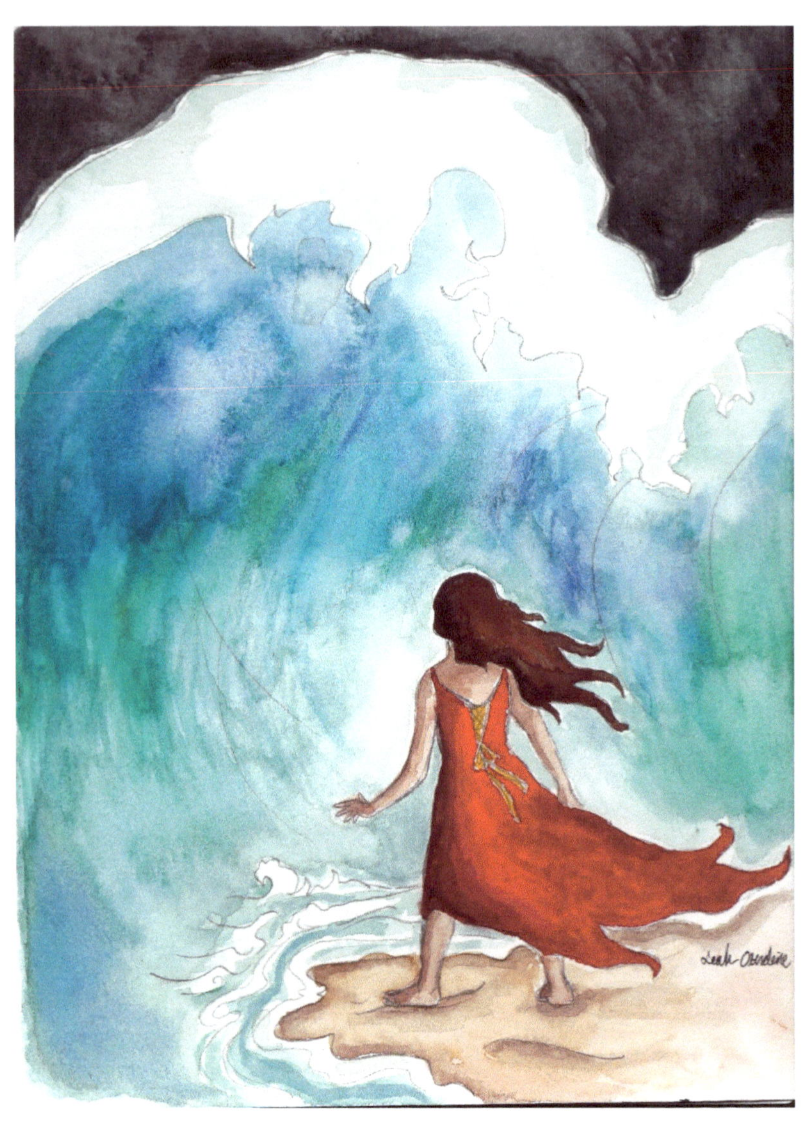

a storm called liberation

Fallen, my blood seeps into the ground.
Blinded, my mind hijacked and confounded.

I tried to destroy my own soul,
I listened to my own lies.
Bound in a tangle of darkness,
my throat raw from the screams and cries.

Resurrected, my wounds cleansed
and purified by the Creator,
Eyes wide open; I take hold of the clarity
and power He bestows.

Snapped me out of my delusions,
cut the ties that held me trapped and lost.
Keep telling yourself a lie,
and soon it becomes the truth.

God is not the author of confusion,
He gives direction on what to do.
Throw off the ropes, shred the lies like paper,
toss them to the wind.

Your feet weren't meant to be stagnant,
your mind wasn't made to sleep.
Pick your body off the floor,
plant your feet firm and grit your teeth.

In Him, you will overcome, you will survive,
and you will find peace.
There's a reason for this tempest,
this hurricane is only one of many.

The torrent of emotions is only a season,
and you're strong enough, you won't drown.
You're in a refining fire and in the end you will be like silver,
if you fully seek the Lord.

This tribulation will free you,
brace yourself and stand your ground.
Freedom isn't a gentle thing,
liberation takes you by storm.

So throw your chains away;
allow the flood to envelop your soul.
You will bleed, you will plead for the end to come.

The darkness of night only points
to our need for the sun.
I see clouds on the horizon,
but I am thankful for the storms.

Lighting illuminates the heavens;
thunder rolls like an orchestral score.
Focus on the prize ahead,
and think to the years of the future,
When, tried by the fire, having weathered the turbulence,
having done all to stand,

your skin will be thicker, your mind wiser,
and your feet closer to the Promised Land.

bleed in secret

Oh, I'm falling down,
Oh, I feel alone.
Oh, I need some help 'cause,
I can't do this on my own.

Find myself running,
Trying to get away.
From everything around me,
I try to hide my face.

Don't want them to see me crying;
Can't let them see the tears.
Don't want them to know I'm suffering;
They don't need to know my fears.

Abba, Father, I need You;
No one else would understand.
No one sees the hurt within me;
You alone can see within.

You know my heart is breaking,
I feel it ripping apart.
But Father, please, I beg you,
Don't let the world see my bleeding heart.
Don't let *my* suffering become *their* suffering.

Oh please, let it stop right with me.

While I ache and endure this hardship,
Let it be as if they never knew
What I am going through.

comprehension

You may not understand why
The darkness finds its way in.
Why your mind becomes cloudy and numb,
Or why your bones feel tired and stiff

You may not understand why
The sadness eats at your heart.
Why it devours you like a piece of bread,
Or why the fear tears you apart

You may not understand why
The tears trickle down your face.
Why your eyes are wet when they shouldn't be,
Or why it's so hard to smile and be okay.

But you don't have to understand why
Black clouds come and then they go.
Just listen, tomorrow will be much better,
And it's okay that you don't really know.

this heart is his heart

So many times I've found myself
thinking of someone other than my Father.
Instead of serving Him the best I can,
I give my heart away, rather.

Why do I desire what is not mine to want?
I know I have no need.
For the Lord God has provided so well for me,
His Word I know I should heed.

For this heart is not mine to give away;
This heart belongs to the Lord.
For this heart is not mine, but it is His;
I'll give it away no more.

scars

You don't have to erase
The pain, the memories, the regret.
Some things take time to fade;
Open wounds that haven't healed yet.

God knows I brought it on myself,
I can't forget about my past.
But I'm thankful to move on;
Just moving on is more than I could ask.

inheritance lost

Burdened: that's my heart,
My feelings have been sifted through from the start.
I shiver at any thought
Of eternity, and my own walk.

Joyless: that's me within,
I try to work up a smile,
So that I don't appear so grim;
But sadder still, that's just what I am.

Terrified: that's my mind,
That's what makes me cry.
Shall I be covered, will I be alright?
Or will I be judged, cast down, away from all light?

Uncertain: that's my faith,
Cause even though I have been "saved",
I worry that something's in the way;
Am I not doing enough? Oh I dread that coming Day…

Condemnation: that fills my mind,
And this must be why I have cried.
The devil had really worked and tried
To make me stumble and waste precious time.

Letting go: that's me now;

I'll go back to the Word, I will not stall.
I know I am redeemed, no more will I fall,
Listening to Satan's deceiving lull.

Set free: that is me;
Now that I have chosen to believe.
What Jesus said, what I now see,
His promises I willingly receive.

Condemnation: won't put me down, I am made new;
I cast aside the lies that scream "your works must get you through".
Because I know my works never can, never will.
My inheritance lost? No, His salvation is with me true.

ghosts, or memories?

A white car driving down Klosterman Ave,
It's not really there, but I still visualize it.
I was in that car on Klosterman Ave,
The ghosts are only memories of a season past.

Such a strange sensation, so detached, like a dream,
To see myself on the beach chair, at eighteen.
Two years have passed, but it seems like yesterday,
The memories are like tattoos that you can't rub away.

My past floats in front of me like a vapor;
I watch it like a rerun of an old TV show.
Even though I see it myself, it's a different girl than I,
Emerging from chrysalis, she leaves her old shell behind.

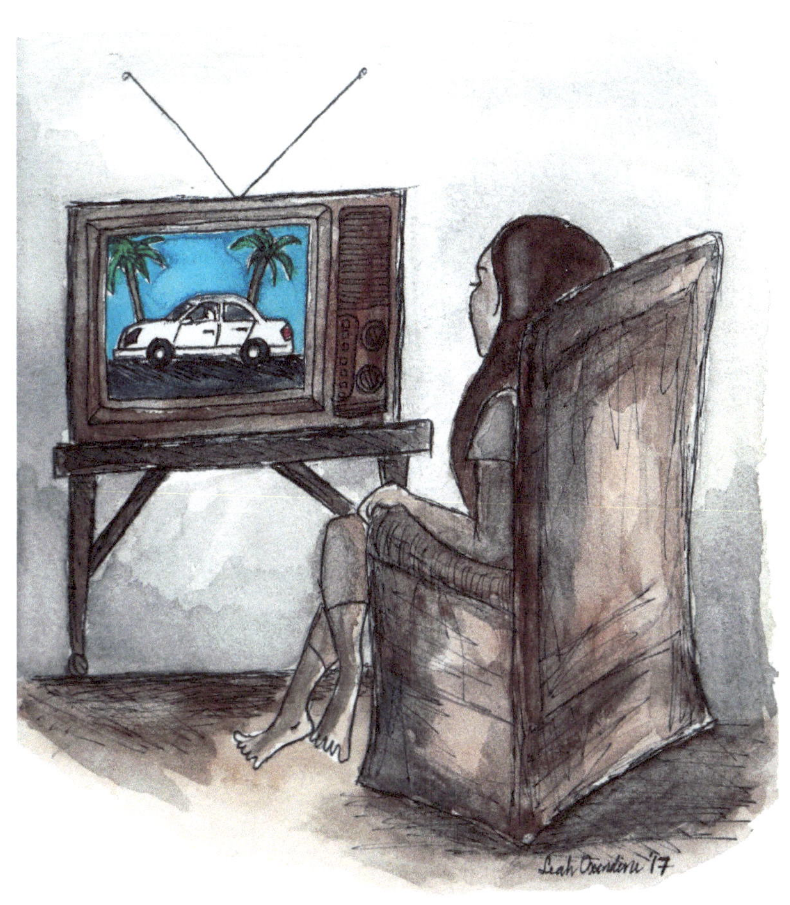

heartbreaker

I understand
You're hurt and you say it's all me.
I can imagine
That it's hard for you to move on.
But listen
I didn't want to make this choice.
And realize
Staying would have just hurt you more.

I understand
Why you blame me for your heartache.
I can imagine
How you would think I'm a vile thing.
But listen
I never wished for your sadness.
And realize
I had to be true to myself

the scars of vivid humanity

PART III

essence of humanity

Eyes lacking vigor, hands drained of life,
A mouth that only utters empty promises and lies.
Aggression leaves its mark in the lines on our faces;
Some days we're proud of them, and some days we hate it.

I run, but it's not from someone else I try to hide.
I cry, but it's not from the rolling thunder in the night sky.
I fight, but it's not against a person the eyes can behold,
It's against that blue-eyed girl staring back in the mirror.

We have good days and bad, but deep down we're always searching
For an answer to a question that's beyond our understanding.
'Cause the pain inside won't go away, without some kind of remedy,
And when we try to fix it ourselves, the medicine only turns to poison.

Who knew the greatest enemy, could be the essence of humanity,
And at our greatest, we just amount to failure.
Can't you see the pain that we're all trying to hide?
Do you understand the mighty torrent raging deep inside?

On earth, where can I find the remedy?
If it were here, wouldn't it be clear to see?

Earth provides not solutions - just clues, pointing Above, subtle signs
And the essence of humanity overlooks them all the time.

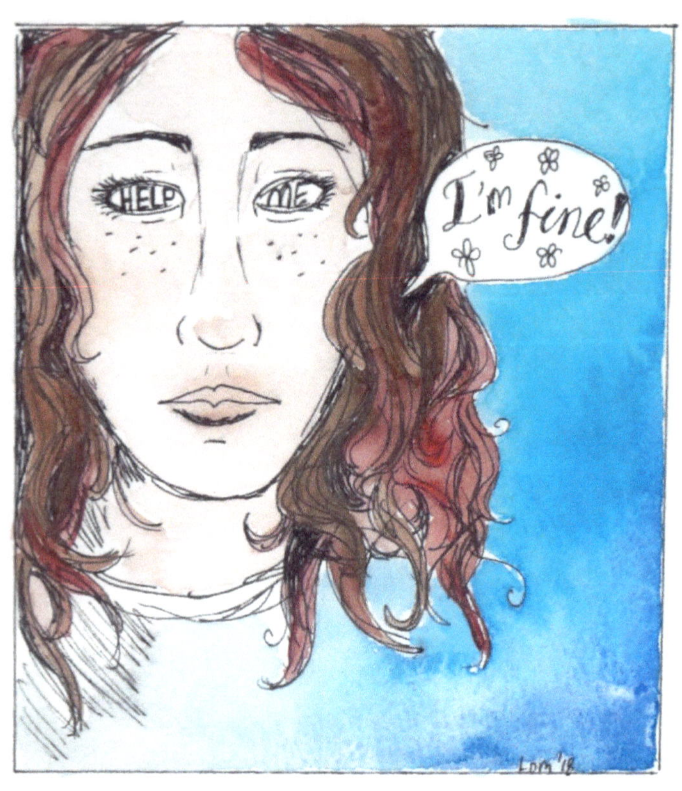
HELP
ME
I'm fine!

Turquoise eyes
speak volumes untold.
Beyond their glassy surfaces
are dreams and longings,
another world.

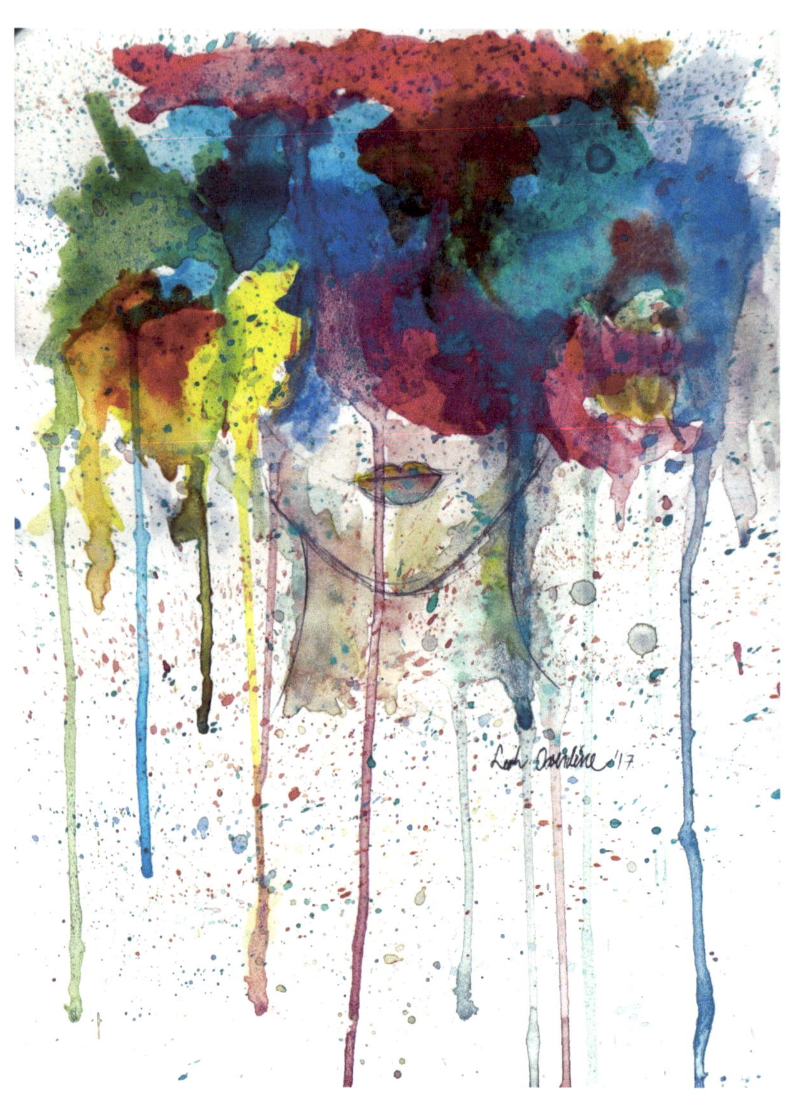

stares

I sit here, defenseless, powerless,
Unable to make you cease.
Apparently,
You're captivated with me,
Wish I could make you stop.

You pierce me with your eyes,
You penetrate, I despise.
Wishing I could take your stare,
And push it far away from me elsewhere.
Anywhere.

You make my insides crawl,
You drive me up the wall.
You know it ain't polite?
When you watch me like a hawk,
When will you learn to stop?

I probably shouldn't care,
I try to make myself forget.
What's a little incessant stare, they say,
What's a little gaze that never ends?
Everything.

Stop devouring me with your gaze,
You'll never win my heart this way.

I’m not an exhibit for you to examine,
So wishing I could take your stare,
And push it far away,
Elsewhere.

augmented harmony (if love burns)

If love is composed of lightning and thunder,
If love comes like a hurricane,
If love burns me like a refining fire,
Lord, please don't spare me from the flames.

If I suffer and I bleed, I know it's not in vain.
If I lose all that I was, I'll still withstand the rain.
If this is why I'm here, for such a time as this,
If wisdom spawns from pain, then show me what I've missed.

If love is peaceful like a breeze in the summer night,
If love comes quiet, slow and shy,
If love is an ocean deep, I want it to encompass me,
I'd rather drown, than leave its waves tonight.

If love is worth fighting for, I'll be the first to draw my sword,
If love means leaning on Your word.
If life is a melody, then trials are its harmony,
And it's a vibrant song I'm glad I learned.

Like a balsam I'll stand straight and tall,
I will rise up every time I fall.

I'll never break, though I may bend – this season now is not the end.

the power of now

Time is perception,
Perception is relative.
Moments are fleeting,
Time is deceiving.

When a child, the days are slow,
They speed up as you grow old.
When enough breaths have passed,
The pace slows; one breath becomes your last.

Some souls grow young, while others grow old,
Wisdom isn't measured by the number you hold.
Time is relative, but numbers are not.
Time vanishes now as you give this thought.

There is no future, there is only now.
For now is the future, and the future is now.
Today is yesterday's future, tomorrow's past,
The present is a vapor that cannot last.

Open your eyes, open your mind.
This very minute is a gift.
How many precious minutes will you miss,
Before taking hold of the power of *now*?

soundwaves are my canvas

I paint pictures with my fingers on the fret board of my guitar.
Craft stories with big words on the blank spaces of white papers.
I got paintbrushes for hands; a blender full of lightning for a brain
I might look harmless to you, but how harmless is a hurricane?

Not sure if it's the green tea running rampant through my veins,
Or the many thoughts and visions that float past my eyes each day.
But my purpose seems so clear and defined,
Branded on my soul like galaxies in a winter night sky.

You'd be deaf, you'd be blind,
If you can't hear, can't see the colors in my mind.
But you'd be crazy, you'd be insane,
If you could ever understand, comprehend my brain.

I paint pictures with sound,
And every instrument's my friend.
Sound waves are my canvas, and words, my satisfaction.
I dream in different languages and live in vibrant worlds

I'm on a locomotive that makes entirely no sense,
Speeding down the highway and writing in the past tense.
There's a reason they tell me to avoid the caffeine,
Cause' I'm already just as crazy as can be.

You'd be deaf, you'd be blind,

If you can't hear, can't see the colors in my mind.
You'd be crazy, you'd be insane,
If you could understand, comprehend my brain.

The creative tribe's got a crazy vibe,
Our craniums are a little
Different
Inside.

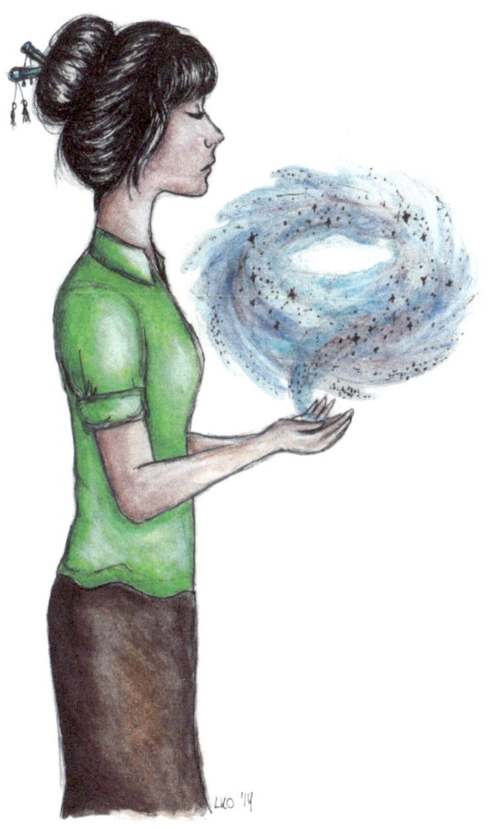

seven billion

Coffee brown skies and coal black sidewalks,
Yellow taxicabs racing down the street.
Millions of people brushing past me,
And I forget whether I'm coming or going.

Welcome to New York City,
Welcome to a hurting land.
The neon lights are burning bright, but
They can't hide the darkness thriving here.

Seven billion people on planet earth
Seven billion lives of incredible worth.
Seven billion people in this world,
How many of seven billion have truly heard?

How many lives have been touched?
By hands reaching out, spreading God's Holy Word?
How many souls have been told the Good News?
How they can be saved from hell and what Jesus can do?

Seven billion, that's a pretty huge number,
But the Lord made us all unique and special.
Children of God, we've been given a task,
To spread the gospel to as many as we can.

Towering pine trees and fields of green,
Prettiest landscape that I ever did see.
Horse farms scattered all across the county
Rolling down the road, pick-up trucks and dualees.

Welcome to Fairfield, Florida,
Welcome to a needy land.
The stars, they shine in the clear night sky,
But they can't hide the darkness dwelling here.

What are we doing, standing here,
Drowning in the waters of our own fears?
Why do we worry what others think?
Why do we let that worry stop us from witnessing?

Why do we worry about others' thoughts?
When we step outside our comfort zones,
We step into God's.

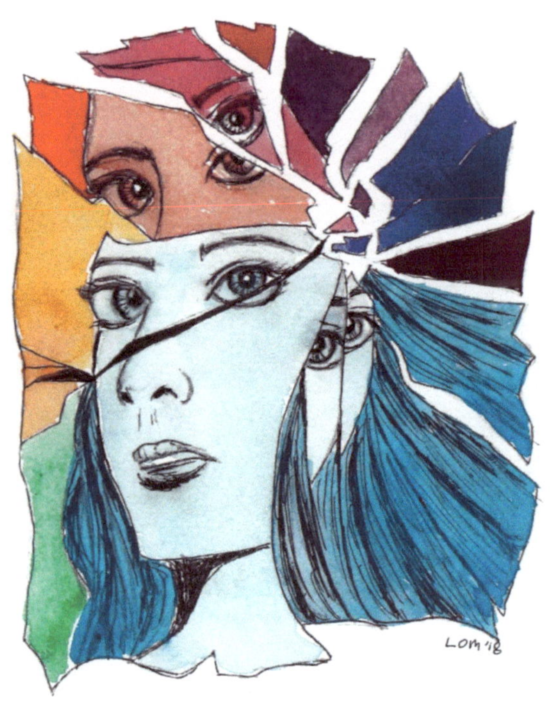
LOM '18

these walls

These walls house two people, and the two people don't get along.
These walls house two enemies, and they wage war, oh they wage war.
Welcome to a morbid home, these walls are covered in blood;
Welcome to a battleground, a less-than-peaceful abode.

These windows are clouded, because the people always fight.
These windows are a mirror to the darkness and the light.
What a pity, what a shame. You wouldn't understand their little game.
They're fighting to get out, and if you listen close you can hear them.

Between these blue eyes you see,
There's an entire world underneath.
And beneath this convincing smile,
There's a scheming crocodile.
Inside this cranium, inside this heart,
There's no vacancy, that's for sure.

Would you run if you knew, that behind these eyes of blue,
These walls hide more than one mind, and there's a war, oh there's a war inside?
Would you think that I'm a freak, if all within me were to speak,
Would you run if you could see, that there are *really* two of me?

I told her to get lost, there's no room in this little house.
But she said she has a plan of her own, and these walls can't hold us both.
So I drew my sword and she drew hers, and we fought it out right there.
We painted the walls with blood, oh, in our morose abode.

These windows are tinted, so nobody can look within.
They'd see two girls fighting in a symphony of sin.
These windows are a portal to a chaotic world below.
Sometimes it's beautiful, and sometimes it's a warzone.

Between these eyes of cerulean,
There's a struggle to be free.
And behind this sun-kissed face,
Is another girl in another space.
No vacancy in this heart, no room in this mind,
Too many occupants fighting for time.

Would you run if you knew, that behind these eyes of blue,
These walls house more than one mind, and there's a war, oh there's a war inside?
Would you think that I'm a freak, if all within me were to speak,
Would you run if you could see, that there are really two of me?

And would it scare you to know, that I've embraced it so?
These walls house two of us, and we're rising from the dust.
When we aren't fighting, we are strong – we create the harmony in our song.
When I stretch my wings, look to the sky, because it takes the two of us to fly.

This is a strange little house, a strange little heart.
But sometimes the occupants paint brilliant works of art.
There is gold amid the crimson; stars in the darkened night,
Because together, when our minds are one, we are victors in our fight.

Be full of optimism,

and you will be full

of sunshine.

bedtime

Blackness envelops me again,
I soak my bed with a river of tears.
I try to imagine him lying there beside me,
But he is so far away, he is not here.

The loneliness surrounds me again,
I squeeze my pillow ever so tight.
I try to pretend he is holding me in his arms,
But he is so far away, nowhere in sight.

The sadness impales me again,
I curl into a ball, hugging my knees.
I try to count down the days till we are together,
But it is easier just to cry myself to sleep.

The choice to be content in all things
is like being in the eye of the hurricane.
You are surrounded by havoc,
but it cannot touch you.

homesick

For most of my life,
I prayed I would find true love.
And life took me by surprise,
When you came along.

Never thought I could feel
Quite the way you make me feel.
You bring me joy when you're here,
And my heart breaks when you're away.

When I was young I would dream
Of being with someone like you.
And I learned that God answers prayers,
And that dreams really do come true.

We never have enough time,
Our adventures never last long enough.
I've never felt more alive,
But my soul aches when you are away.

I've learned that home is more
Than walls and rooftops and doors.
I'm not homesick for a place,
I'm homesick for your soul.

The act of being negative is like having a garden of beautiful flowers and watering them with bleach.

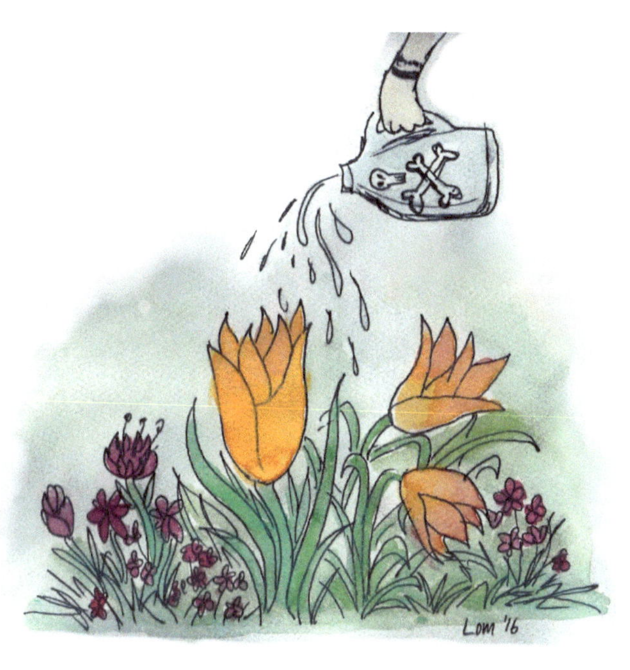
Lom '16

The act of seeing yourself in the mirror and seeing a reflection you despise is like being angry because you were given the world and not the universe.

It brings me the nicest feeling being aware that the approval of the world is not needed for me to be radiant.

Do you ever long to be somewhere that's not a place and do you desire something that is not a thing? Did you ever think that your true home was not a house, but someone's soul?

wandering galaxies

I’m drawn to the sparkling lights,
Drenching my soul in the sea of stars.
Your eyes glitter in the night,
My spirit soars above the blanket of trees

I don’t need wings to take flight and rise,
To leave my body here on earth.
You squeeze my hand, looking into the skies,
We become one with the wandering galaxies above.

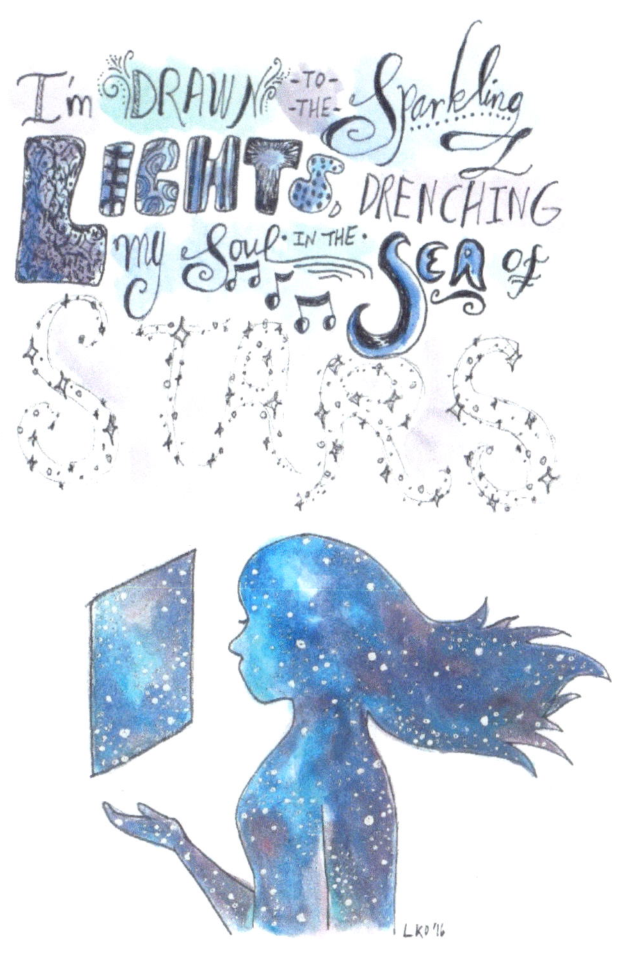
I'm DRAWN -TO- -THE- Sparkling
LIGHTS, DRENCHING
my Soul · IN THE · SEA of
STARS
LKO '16

life through your eyes

Here I go, falling down again, I mess up, and I shake my head.
This was not the way it was to go. I give up, it's out of my control.
Why do things have to go this way? Why can't it just be a better day?

Time flies by, and I'm left in the dust, so much more to do before I bust.
Not enough hours in my day, but I guess there's nothing else to say.
Why do things have to go this way? Why can't it just be a better day?

Imperfection is my middle name, and every day, it's the same.
It's no secret, I can't beat it, I am broken, I'm outspoken.
Imperfection is my middle name, Lord, I need you to turn around this day.

My world is crashing down on me, everything that I thought was complete.
All my plans just crumbled on the floor, and I give up just like I've done before.
Why do things have to go this way? Why can't it just be a better day?

Help me see blessings that You have bestowed on me.

Help me to look at every day as a chance, an opportunity.
To bless others, to love others, to glorify Your name.
To walk with You, to grow in You, each and every day.

It doesn't have to get any easier; just let me see it through your eyes.
Help me see the good in everything, help me understand what Your will is for me.
Help me know that I am not alone. O Lord, guide me in the way You want me to go.

separate ways

My heart would beat a bit faster,
I would swallow, blink my eyes.
At thinking about you, or hearing about you,
This I did, I'll admit, sometimes.

I never could help it,
But that's just the way it went.
It's not like I liked it,
Not how I wanted my emotions spent.

My heart broke once, twice,
Will it break again?
Not if I can help it,
I won't let it break again.

So we went our separate ways,
I don't know you anymore.
Our minds live in separate states,
Because I knew something else was in store.

And despite all the memories in my head,
I've gotten past the fact.
You aren't in my life anymore
And this train's on a better track.

in the arms of grace

Walking along, I feel so good, everything seems to be as it should.
The sky is bright, my dreams are in sight, I'm just glad to be alive!

You know, when they say you're in the clouds,
When everywhere you look around, all is bright, all is beautiful.

Everything seems to fall in place,
When you're resting in the arms of grace.

Maybe this is what joy feels like
Maybe this is what hope feels like
Maybe this is what peace feels like
Maybe this is what grace feels like.

I feel those arms around me now, they give me joy too great to tell.
You know I never felt this way, until Jesus saved the day.

Jesus loves me this I know, without Him, I'd be all alone.
As He extends His hand, I know He's got a plan.

Everything will always fall in place,
When you're resting in the arms of grace.

to michael

We are a two-piece puzzle,
You and I.
We fit together perfectly,
Side by side.

We are two hearts,
That blended into the same.
I love that we share so much,
And that soon I will share your name.

the proposal

This is the beautiful story
Of what happened on a cool April night.
On the battlefield of Shiloh, Tennessee,
Under the ball tent's sparkling lights.

She was playing bodhran with the band,
He smiled, nervously watching from the side.
For scarce did the young lady know,
That he would ask her to be his bride.

The magic began when he spoke the words,
Telling of his deep love for the girl.
And tears streamed down her face,
For she loved him more than any other in the world.

Of course, she nodded yes, with no hesitation,
For it was all of her dreams come to pass.
And their spirits laughed, their hearts danced,
For they had found their true love at long last.

the vividness of you

Feed me the nectar of your lips,
Give me the velvet touch of your kiss.

Don't get me high unless it's on you,
Don't indulge me unless it's on your love.

All the colors lose their hues,
Compared with the vividness of you.

more sappy love poetry

My love, I need you
Like the air I breathe.
You are the oxygen
That fills my lungs.

Craving you more
Than words can speak.
Each day without you is
As a thousand years.

falling in love

Inhaling the stars tonight,
Never felt quite this way.
Never been more alive,
Never been more afraid.

Afraid to exhale, to blink my eyes,
Fearing the daybreak when the moon leaves.
Never been more awake,
While the rest of the earth sleeps.

when i save a spider's life

When I save a spider's life,
A sparkle lights my eyes.
For I know I've done a service,
To the hated arachnid kind.

When I save a spider's life,
I cannot help but grin.
You may say I'm demented,
But I feel spiders are my kin.

it's a beautiful thing

written in honor of my best friend Maygan's wedding

A small town girl and a country guy,
A church picnic on a winter's night.
Everybody dancin' a reel or two,
It was the start of something glorious that no one yet knew

She saw him standin' there, lookin' real shy,
So she asked him to dance, tryin' to be nice.
A friendship bloomed, and time flew by,
Under a starry night sky, he asked her to be his bride.

It's a beautiful thing,
When two hearts join together.
It's a beautiful story,
When two souls commit to forever.
When a guy and a girl who love the Lord, and walk according to His Word,
Find each other, give all for the other,
It's a beautiful thing.

She's a curly-haired musician, loves to draw and sing,
He's a tall mechanic, he can fix most anything.
She's always barefoot, he's always got his boots,
Glued to each other, you can't separate them two.

Two kindred spirits, on a new page of life.
Together they will go far, their story shining bright.
When you start to wonder if beautiful stories still exist,
Just look at those two God-fearing country kids.

Happily ever after is just a phrase in a fairy tale,
But sometimes in life, real life's better than the dream.
It don't have to be all perfect and according to plan,
Cause' true love ain't defined by the notions of man.

our song

Darling, let's go stare at the stars—Take my hand in yours, 'cause that's where it belongs.
Just looking into your eyes, hope I can say all that needs to be said—Darling, I promise
I'll love you 'till the end.
Darling, look, they're waltzing now—Take my hand in yours, and let's show them how.
When I'm here, staring into your eyes—Everything feels just right.

Last time I checked the radio, there wasn't a song about us.
All the stuff on the radio couldn't describe our love.
Last time I checked the radio, they got the lyrics all wrong.
So forget all the stuff on the radio, 'cause this is our song.

This is our story, our adventure tale—We don't know the ending yet, who knows when we ever will.
But it's all in the Lord's hands, and that's what matters most—
He's got great things planned for us, I know.
Darling, don't ever change the way you smile—In each season of life, let's go the extra mile.
Let's do amazing things, and praise the King of Kings— and never let our fire falter and fade,
Oh, I'm gonna love you more and more each passing day.

Darling, keep your arms 'round me tight.

Let's live in the moment, never closing our eyes.
Whenever life gets hard, we won't let it lose its flavor.
May we look back on these moments and always remember.

futile fortunes

Money, ambitions, climbing that ladder,
Getting bags under your eyes from all those extra hours.
Living for the weekend and dreading Mondays,
Hoping you'll have enough for the bills to pay.

Money, shiny new cars, the American dream,
Your eyes so tired from staring at that computer screen.
Never really see the family much anymore,
But at least you have an awesome credit score.

Money, big houses, getting on TV,
You've got back pain now, arthritis and a bad knee.
They say you have to sacrifice some things in life,
Time, health or money, you can't have all three.

So give me a little house in the woods,
Give me a husband who will love me as he should.
Give me peace with God, loyal friends and kin,
Because that's the only fortune I wish to win.

banishing fear

Fears doesn't exist in my mind,
When God is by my side, it's alright.
Fears don't carry any weight,
When He's here with me, the devil, the devil has to flee

It's so easy to get caught up in the hurries, the worries,
And each day a new fear carries its burden.
On the radio, the TV shows, the world is falling apart,
The world is going mad, where do we start?

We've got fighting and war from shore to shore,
Thousands of people are dying each day.
From the women's center down the street,
Where a scared teenager in green khakis lies on the operation table,
Soon her baby's life will be no more.

To the starving child across the sea,
Who's living the reality of a nightmarish dream.
Bruised and crying, perishing, dying,
Soon he will enter eternity.

The world is like a slaughter, waiting to devour,
Thirsty to consume lives.
But Jesus, I know that you will right the wrongs,

You won't forget those who are forgotten
And for this, fear has no place in my mind.

threads

Freedom of speech, what does it mean?
Is it a book of rules to read?
Is it just an ideal, of which we dream?
People died for it, yet we cannot speak.

If my beliefs are not approved,
There is no freedom applied to me.
As if my lips had been sewn shut,
Silent, I must watch their hypocrisy.

With a thread of red, white and blue,
My voice is suppressed, stitched closed.
For the sake of not offending,
My opinion is crumpled up and disposed of.

Maybe if I was like one of them,
Maybe if I agreed with what they said,
Maybe they'd remove the threads
That force my thoughts to stay locked in my head.

Maybe...
If I was politically correct...

the box

The Box is where you feel comfortable,
The Box is where you are safe.
The Box is something you don't question,
The Box is always the Right Way.

The Box promises to be predictable,
The Box is what comes natural.
The Box offers everything you want in life,
The Box is always factual.

Outside The Box is another dimension,
Outside The Box is a forbidden planet.
Outside The Box is driving far, far away from home,
And then becoming stranded.

Outside The Box…
Your dreams dance in colors you've never seen,
Your mind thinks thoughts that are truly free,
You understand what is your purpose and meaning.

Do you dare step across the threshold?
The distinction between being a name or a number?
That precarious line between *existing*, and *thriving*?
Perhaps the only fear that constrains you from being you
Is the bleak, powerless shadow of The Box.

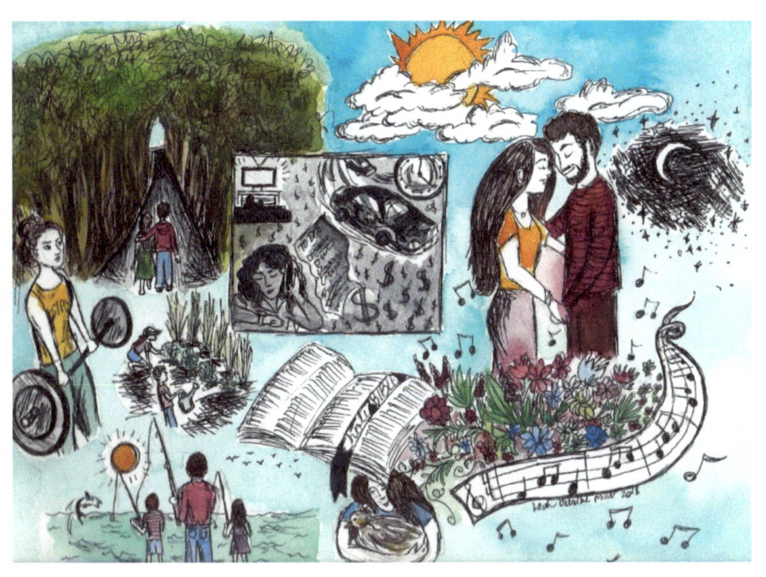

single-minded

Sometimes we continue on in life,
Sometimes we just do what we like.
Forgetting the others who come across
The view from our perceptions.

They go their own way, we go ours,
We seem to forget they existed at all.
As if we didn't see,
They also take part in living.

As we find enjoyment in these days,
When we run and play and shout and sing,
Do we ever truly notice
Who we come across along the way?

But while we stand aside and do our own thing,
Someone out there is suffering.
While we live our lives revolving in our little circles,
When will we ever reach out and break that bubble?

till' the end

So open my eyes and soften my heart,
And from your presence never depart.
I wanna be more like you in all that I do,
I wanna glorify you.

So take over my mind and banish all this pride,
That's been keepin' me from being by your side.
I need a Savior, need a friend,
Who'll be here with me till' the end.

Well everything on this earth has a death, has a birth.
We live, we breathe, we die, we fade, and time goes by so quick each day.
Like a flower swiftly fading, like a blade of grass that's wilting,
Numbered are our days in this world, eternity is soon to unfold.

Even though this earth will dissolve, and the skies and mountains fall,
There is still one who remains, and incorruptible His Name.
Though all we know is fleeting away, there's still someone who will stay,
Mighty Creator, King of Kings, and incorruptible His Name.

The heavens will roll up as a scroll,
And time will be no more.

We'll be in the presence of our Lord,
And time will be no more.

to my future children

Well, here you are, in a world that hates your kind.
Here you will be forced to make up your mind.
Sitting on the fence while others die,
Or actively standing for what is right?

As your mother, I am imperfect, will fail you,
Do not be surprised when I disappoint you.
Where I will disappoint, our Creator does not,
Accept His love and tell Him all of your thoughts.

He will protect you through anything you will face,
Through the persecution, through the world's rage.
If you don't back down from what is right,
Remember that you will overcome the darkness of the night.

I give you my word to do the very best I can,
Preparing you for life, always extending a loving hand.
So that no matter what you do, wherever you go,
You'll be ready for anything, and of God's promises, you'll always know.

perfect romance

I remember you standing there, looking so fine.
You had the most beautiful smile in your eyes.
Right then and there, I realized a thing—You changed me.
I let my bitter heart learn to love.

Can't always know, time doesn't show,
Doesn't always reveal what's meant to be.
But I'll give it a chance, a second glance,
Because, dear, something tells me you're my perfect romance.

I remember you stood out, weren't like the crowd.
Unlike all the others, you stood so proud.
You stole my heart, and ever since then—Each time I see you again,
I swear my icy heart melts more and more.

Never thought I'd be the one to say this,
With all I've been through.
But with you by my side, I feel I'm in heaven,
And the sky is always blue.

a whole lot of you and me

A little bit of sugar, A little bit of honeysuckle.
A little bit of front porch swing, and how you make my heart sing.
A whole lot of amazing grace, and feeling the sunshine on my face.
A little bit of cold sweet tea, And a whole lot of you and me.
You and me.

Well some folks need their fancy cars and mansions,
I guess that's fine for them, but not for me.
They can have their fancy cars and mansions,
But the simple things in life are all I need.

Some things can't be bought and can't be sold,
And love is so much more than currency.
Well, all I know is, what's the point of gold,
If it all it does is take away your peace?

Well, yes life has its share of ups and downs.
Sometimes the silver lining is hard to see.
But even with its share of ups and downs,
There's always at least one good memory .

They say our love is too good to be true,
'Cause people come and go like seasons past.
But they don't really know me or you,
'Cause our romance, it was built to last.

There's not much that I need in this world.
And there's not much that I want from this earth.
All I really need, is you beside me,
And the Good Lord who put you in my life.

a splash of cold water

Alone,
Close to Your throne.
Nothing I'd like but to be with You.

Together,
From the start, and forever.
You never leave, You're always so true.

Away,
In Your Arms I'll stay.
Oh, I never want to leave You.

Give,
Let me live.
Abiding in Your joy, in Your peace.

You,
Just us two.
Together in the quiet, the secret.

Refresh,
Encourage, lift up my head.
Refresh me like a splash of cold water.

retrospect

Some people say
Take me back to the
"good old days".
Their minds only
Dwell on yesterday.

My yesterday? It was my hell.
Yesterday had silver linings,
But the present outshines them all.
Dwelling on yesterday
Means dwelling on what I am not

The girl you saw five years ago,
The woman standing here now.
The girl was surviving on silver linings,
The woman, she feasts on life.
She takes each moment and thrives.

Retrospect.

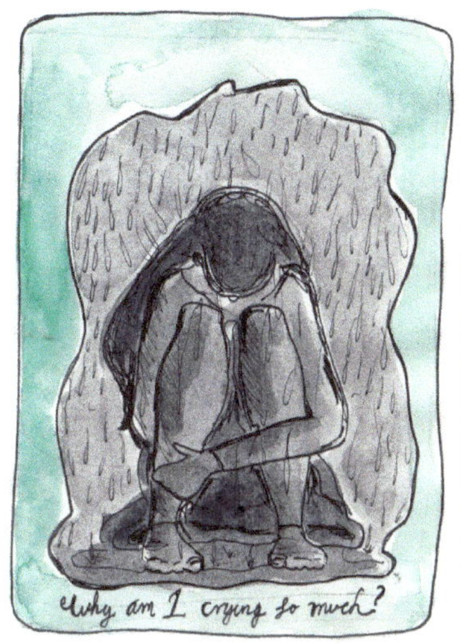
Why am I crying so much?

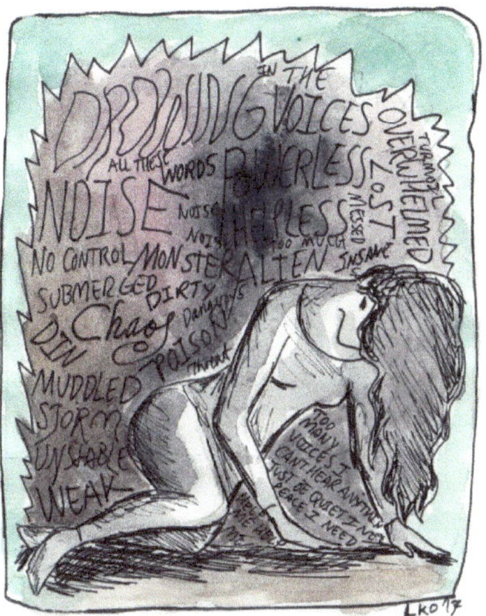
DROWNING IN THE VOICES
ALL THESE WORDS
NOISE
POWERLESS
HELPLESS
LOST
MESSED
OVERWHELMED
TURMOIL
TOO MUCH
INSANE
NO CONTROL
MONSTER
ALIEN
SUBMERGED
DIRTY
DANGEROUS
Chaos
DIN
POISON
THREAT
MUDDLED
STORM
UNSTABLE
WEAK
TOO MANY VOICES I CAN'T HEAR ANYTHING
JUST BE QUIET I NEED PEACE
LKO '17

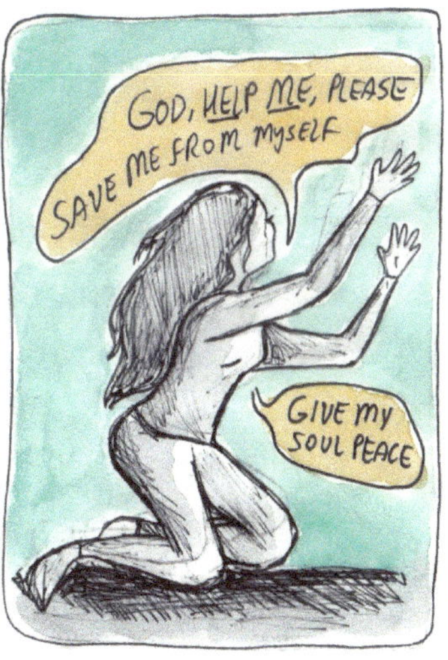
GOD, HELP ME, PLEASE SAVE ME FROM MYSELF
GIVE MY SOUL PEACE

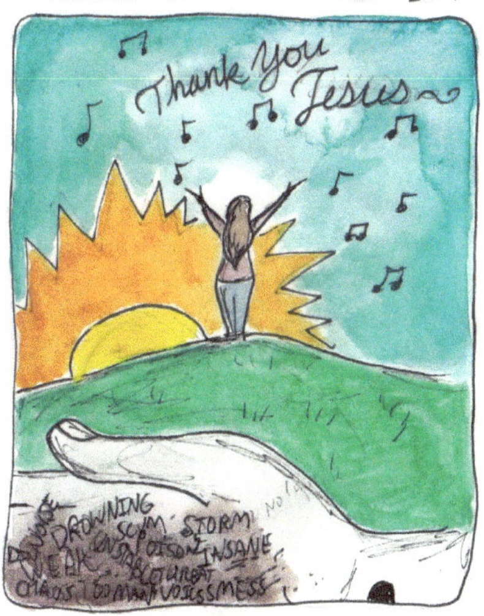
Thank You Jesus
DROWNING
STORM
INSANE
WEAK
CHAOS
MESS

breathe

Inhale.
Allow your mind to drift,
Take your thoughts to a place beyond yourself.
And just breathe.

Exhale.
Your bones release a sigh of gratitude,
As you feel the warmth of the floor beneath you.
Just be.

Inhale.
Reward yourself with this moment.
As your body melts into a sea of calm.
Let go.

Exhale.
Embrace the solitude that cushions you.
Slowly return to the world of the present.
And be free.

the voyage

The anticipation.
The reality.
The fear of the unknown.
Leaving the familiar behind.
The joy of new beginnings.
The adventure.
The struggle.
This earth-shattering journey starts
Now.

about the author

Leah K. Oxendine (Miller) has been writing, drawing and creating ever since she was little. In 2017, she published her first historical fiction novel, *The Rebels of Florida*. Now 22, she is happily married to the love of her life, Michael. She enjoys presenting living history demonstrations at American Civil War reenactments and speaking about Florida history at local events. She is passionate about music and can play nine different instruments, including piano, which is her favorite. She lives to glorify God in all that she does. Leah is also a certified personal trainer and group fitness instructor. She is especially fond of tea, candles, lifting weights, exploring the great outdoors, cooking, yoga and spending time with friends and family!

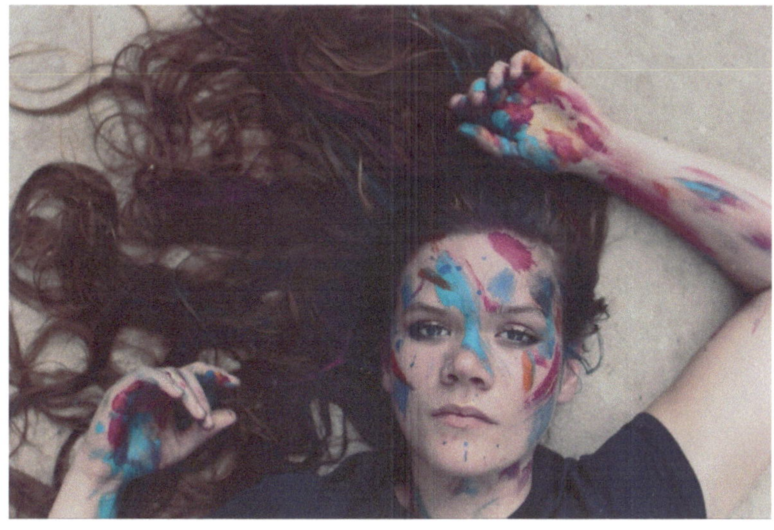

WEBSITE - www.leahoxendine.com
INSTAGRAM - @leah_oxendine_strong
FACEBOOK - www.facebook.com/whenmysoulbleedswords

www.ingramcontent.com/pod-product-compliance
Lightning Source LLC
LaVergne TN
LVHW052253100826
845147LV00001B/37

* 9 7 8 0 5 7 8 4 0 2 3 2 1 *